8/29/92

DISCARD

PICTURE LIBRARY

SNOW SPORTS

PICTURE LIBRARY
SNOW SPORTS

Norman Barrett

Franklin Watts

London   New York   Sydney   Toronto

© 1987 Franklin Watts

First published in Great Britain
    1987 by
Franklin Watts
12a Golden Square
London W1R 4BA

First published in the USA by
Franklin Watts Inc
387 Park Avenue South
New York
N.Y. 10016

First published in Australia by
Franklin Watts
14 Mars Road
Lane Cove
2066 NSW

UK ISBN: 0 86313 514 5
US ISBN: 0-531-10353-6
Library of Congress Catalog Card
Number 86-51226

Printed in Italy

Designed by
Barrett & Willard

Photographs by
All-Sport
All-Sport/Vandystadt
N.S. Barrett Collection
    (historical)

Illustration by
Rhoda & Robert Burns

Technical Consultant
Howard Bass

Contents

Introduction

People enjoy snow sports in many parts of the world. Skiing is widely popular both as a leisure activity and as a competitive sport. There are all kinds of skiing events and ski jumping is a thrilling spectacle. Other snow sports include tobogganing and bobsledding.

Several snow sports are included in the Winter Olympics, held every four years.

△ A ski racer rounds a pole in a slalom event. In slalom, the competitors weave in and out of pairs of poles called gates on a short downhill course. This kind of racing is part of Alpine skiing.

6

Skiing can be divided into two main types, Nordic and Alpine. Nordic skiing comes from northern Europe. It is cross-country skiing, but also includes ski jumping and biathlon, a mixture of skiing and shooting.

Alpine skiing comes from the Alps, a range of mountains in Europe. The competitive Alpine events are downhill racing, giant slalom and slalom. Mountain touring on skis is a popular leisure activity.

△ Competitors in a ski marathon take some refreshment during the race. In some places, such as Scandinavia and Canada, thousands of people take part in these long-distance Nordic events.

The ski jump

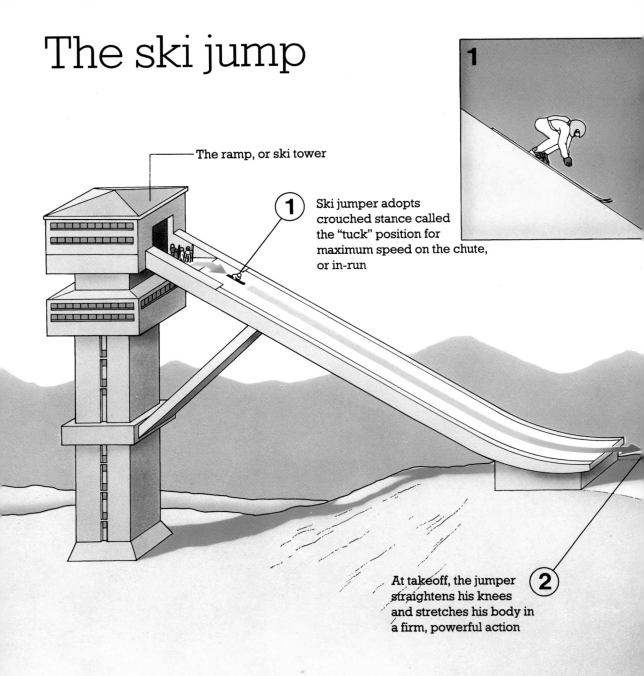

1

The ramp, or ski tower

1 Ski jumper adopts crouched stance called the "tuck" position for maximum speed on the chute, or in-run

2 At takeoff, the jumper straightens his knees and stretches his body in a firm, powerful action

Ski jumpers earn points for the way they jump as well as for how far they jump. Competitors are judged from the moment they take off to when they reach the out-run. Flight through the air and landing are judged for style, control and accuracy.

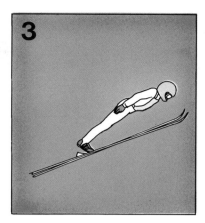

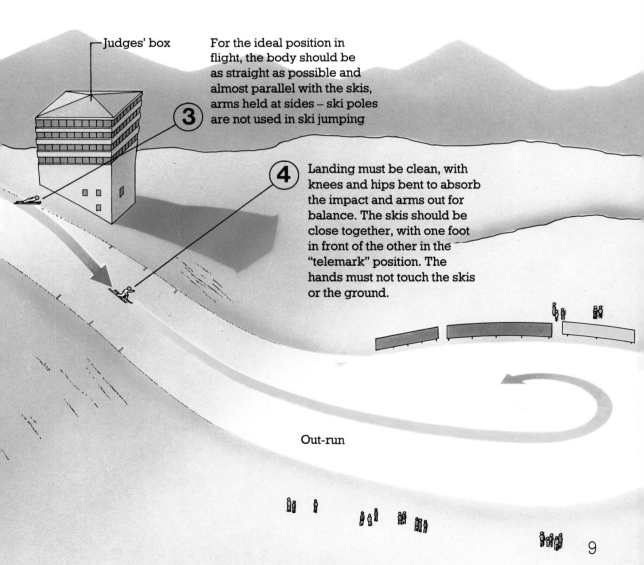

Judges' box

For the ideal position in flight, the body should be as straight as possible and almost parallel with the skis, arms held at sides – ski poles are not used in ski jumping

③

④ **Landing must be clean, with knees and hips bent to absorb the impact and arms out for balance. The skis should be close together, with one foot in front of the other in the "telemark" position. The hands must not touch the skis or the ground.**

Out-run

Skiing

Skiing is great fun. Skiers glide quietly down the slopes, enjoying the spectacular mountain scenery. They keep warm in special ski wear under a bright sun.

Ski resorts have "easier" slopes where beginners can learn the basics of skiing – the "straight run", or "glide," and the simple turns. Learners progress to the "more difficult" and "most difficult" runs.

△ Beginners practicing simple ski movements on gentle slopes. Ski lifts, as seen on the right of the picture, take people to the top of a ski run.

▷ Ski racers using a chairlift to get to the top of the race course. Although Alpine ski races rarely take more than about two minutes to complete, the vertical "drop" might be as much as 3,300 ft (1,000 m).

▽ A group of children receive coaching from a qualified instructor. Dark glasses or goggles are worn as protection against the sun, which can be dangerous when reflected off the snow.

Downhill racing

In downhill racing, competitors take a "set course" from start to finish. They race separately and each run is timed. The racer with the fastest time is the winner.

Downhill racers use their ski poles to pick up speed at the start and for balance at turns. They aim to keep their skis as flat as possible on the snow.

▽ Downhill jumps are spectacular, but racers take to the air only when they have to because of the bumpy nature of a downhill course. They can control their skis far better, and go faster, when they are in contact with the snow.

▷ A downhill racer uses his poles at the start to gather speed. As he leaves the starting gate, he triggers an automatic timing device.

▽ In downhill racing, skiers adopt a stance called the "tuck" position. This reduces the air resistance and helps the skiers to go faster.

13

▷ Downhill racing is the fastest of the Alpine ski racing sports. Champion skiers reach speeds of over 90 mph (140 km/h) on the steep, straight parts of the course.

The turns call for great skill and powerful muscles. As can be seen from the picture, taking a turn at fast speed with the minimum of braking puts enormous stress on the legs.

Downhill racers always wear helmets for protection, because falls at such speeds can be very dangerous. The sport demands a great deal of courage.

Slalom

In slalom, competitors race downhill through a series of gates, represented by pairs of poles. The flags on the gates are alternately red and blue.

There are three types of events, slalom, giant slalom and super-G. Slalom has many gates and tight turns. Giant slalom has fewer gates and wider turns. Super-G is a combination of giant slalom and downhill races.

△ Negotiating the gates of a slalom course calls for great balance and skill. The leading racers take the gates at more than one a second. Races are won on the fastest time, as in downhill, but a gate missed or taken wrongly means disqualification of the racer. In slalom, the two poles of a gate are either red or blue.

▷ The finish of a giant slalom course. Each flag is set on a pair of poles.

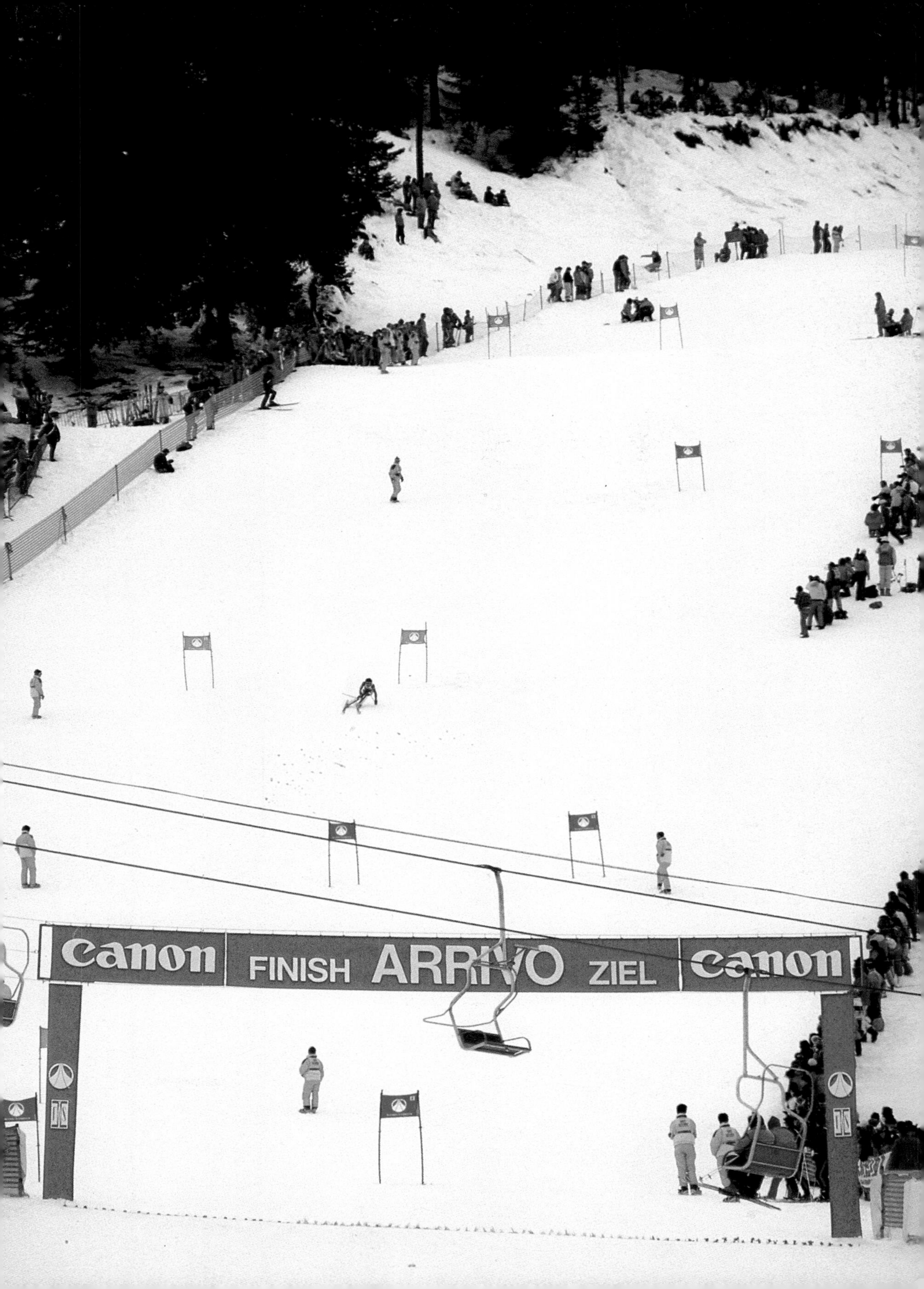
Canon
FINISH ARRIVO ZIEL
Canon

Freestyle

Freestyle is three separate sports. Freestyle ballet is a bit like figure skating on skis. Competitors perform to music on smooth slopes, and are judged on grace and skill.

In aerials, competitors perform mid-air acrobatics off ramps, and points are awarded for style.

In mogul skiing, competitors come down a course covered with moguls, or round bumps. Points are given for turning, speed and overall skill of the run.

▷ Using a special ramp for takeoff, a freestyle skier performs an aerial. Competitors in aerials practice the more difficult acrobatics on trampolines or in water before trying them with skis.

▽ Like aerials, ballet uses gymnastic skills. But it is more graceful, and calls for balance and artistic presentation. Use of the poles is part of the routine.

Cross-country

Nordic, or cross-country, racing requires great stamina. The standard events range from 3 to 30 miles (5 to 50 km), and some marathons are longer. There are fewer sharp turns or steep slopes than there are in Alpine racing.

In the biathlon competitors make stops to shoot at targets. Time penalties are given for missed targets.

△ Looking like an army of ants on the vast white landscape, thousands of marathon skiers wind their way along the valley floor. These mass marathons are held in Europe and North America. Anyone can take part, from champions to beginners.

▷ Ski poles play an important part in cross-country racing. The champion Nordic skiers average about 12 mph (20 km/h). Like long-distance runners, they settle into a rhythmic stride.

▽ Biathlon competitors stop at regular intervals to shoot at targets. During the race, they carry their rifles strapped to their backs.

Ski jumping

Of all the snow sports, ski jumping is the most spectacular. The fearless competitors take off from huge ramps and soar gracefully through the air before landing as much as 330 ft (100 m) away.

There are two ski jumping events, the 70 m and 90 m. These are not the heights of the ramps, or ski towers, but the standard distances expected to be jumped. Points are awarded for style as well as for distance.

▽ High above the ground, like a skydiver without a parachute, a ski jumper looks down on the watching crowd and the town below.

▷ A ski jumper crouches to gather speed as he swoops down the "in run" of a ski tower.

▽ The position in the air (left) is important, and is judged for steadiness and control.

The perfect alignment of the two skis, the correct position of the body and the grace of the ski jumper can best be appreciated from the side (below right).

Other snow sports

Another way of traveling on snow, apart from skis, is on sleds, which have wood or metal runners. There are bobsleds, toboggans and sleds pulled by dogs or horses.

You can sit while skiing – on a skibob. Skiing while being pulled along by a horse or a vehicle is called skijoring. Snowmobiles are motorized snow vehicles, and snowboarding is done on a board instead of two skis.

▽ A bobsled for four people speeds down the course. The pilot, in front, can steer the bob by turning the front runners with a rope or a steering wheel. There are Olympic events for two-people and four-people bobs, on special courses of packed snow and ice. Final standings are decided on the total time for four runs. Speeds of over 90 mph (150 km/h) may be reached.

△ A two-person luge event. Luges are toboggans ridden in a sitting or lying position face-up. They have metal runners but no steering or brakes. There is also a solo luge.

▷ A competitor uses his toe caps to brake a skeleton toboggan. This type of sled is ridden head first and face downward. The major event takes place only on the famous Cresta Run, in Switzerland.

△ A skibob (left), being towed up a ski lift, looks like a bicycle on snow. It has skis instead of wheels. The rider has two small skis, which have claws at the back for braking.

The snowmobile (right) is a motorized sled used for fast snow travel. Special models are built for racing.

◁ Snowboarding, or snowsurfing, is a new sport, a little like surfing in the sea. Competitors race downhill, slalom, and perform freestyle aerials.

▷ Dog-sled racing is popular in the northern parts of North America. Up to nine dogs – huskies or similar breeds – make up a team. Some races last for days and cover hundreds of miles.

▽ Skijoring is a fun sport, like waterskiing on snow. The horses might have riders, or be controlled by the skijorers, as shown here.

The story of snow sports

The first ski race

There is evidence that people used primitive skis in Scandinavia more than 4,000 years ago. But the earliest recorded ski race took place in Norway in 1767. Modern Nordic ski racing developed in the 1880s with the invention of ski bindings.

△ A tobogganing party in the Australian Alps in the early 1900s. Winter sports spread round the world from the European Alps.

American skiing pioneers

Skiing in the United States began in the 1880s in areas where Norwegian populations were found. Goldminers in California began skiing in order to get around the rugged and snowy mountain areas, and the first official ski club in America was formed in La Porte, California, in 1867. Though skiing was primarily regarded as a means of transportation by the miners, it is thought that the goldminers were holding ski races as early as the 1850s.

Sled racing

Sleds have also been a form of winter transport for thousands of years. But it was the British who were responsible for inventing sled sports. British tourists raced sleds down the mountain tracks of the European Alps in the mid-1800s.

From these simple beginnings grew the sports of bobsledding, luge and Cresta Run, or skeleton, tobogganing. These sports caught on and soon spread around the world.

△ A modest form of ski jumping in the 1920s (left) and Birger Rudd (right) of Norway winning the 1936 Olympic ski jumping title.

The Winter Olympics

The first Winter Olympic Games were held at Chamonix, France, in 1924. Nordic ski racing, ski jumping and bobsled were added to the ice skating sports that had been held as part of some previous summer Olympics. Skeleton tobogganing was introduced in 1928, and Alpine ski racing in the 1936 Games. Biathlon became an Olympic sport in 1960, luge tobogganing in 1964.

△ Sulky racing in the snow at St. Moritz, Switzerland, in the 1920s. After the influx of tourists, many resorts became the home of a range of winter sports.

The World Cup

An annual competition known as the World Alpine Ski Cup was first held in 1967. Competitors take part in a series of races held in Europe, North and South America and Japan. They earn points for finishing in the first fifteen in downhill, slalom, giant slalom and super-G races. There are separate men's and women's competitions, and the two people with the most points at the end of the season are the overall winners.

△ The opening ceremony for the 1980 Winter Olympics at Lake Placid, New York, where the 1932 Games were also held.

A safer sport

Skiing has become a much safer sport with the development of improved ski equipment, better ski-trail maintenance and an overall emphasis on skier safety. Ski areas, ski schools and national ski organizations are working to educate skiers so that skiing is a safer sport for everyone.

△ Automatic release safety bindings have made skiing a much safer sport.

Facts and records

△ Jean-Claude Killy.

Olympic champions

Only two men have won all three Alpine racing gold medals at one Olympics. Toni Sailer of Austria won the downhill, slalom and giant slalom titles in 1956, and Jean-Claude Killy of France equaled this feat in 1968. No woman has won more than two.

△ Annemarie Moser.

World Cup queen

Annemarie Moser of Austria won a record six World Cups in the 1970s. The last was in 1979 after she had retired for three years. In 1980 she won her only Olympic gold medal, in the downhill.

△ Specially steamlined helmets and ski suits are worn for speed skiing.

Speed skiing

Speed skiing takes place on specially prepared smooth, steep slopes. Speeds of nearly 130 mph (209 km/h) have been reached over the "flying kilometer."

△ To practice the best position for skiing at high speeds, a skier trains on top of a fast-moving car.

Glossary

Aerials
Acrobatic jumps off a ramp in freestyle skiing.

Alpine skiing
The sport of skiing down mountain slopes.

Ballet
An artistic form of freestyle skiing.

Biathlon
A sport in which cross-country skiers carry rifles and shoot at targets at regular intervals.

Downhill racing
Alpine racing the fastest way down a set course.

Freestyle
A group of skiing sports where points are gained for style.

Gates
Pairs of poles in slalom that the competitor must ski through.

Luge
A toboggan ridden in a sitting or lying-back position.

Mogul
A round bump caused by regular turning of skiers on steep slopes.

Mogul skiing
A freestyle race on a bumpy course in which points are awarded for style as well as time.

Nordic skiing
Cross-country skiing, ski jumping and biathlon.

Skibob
A frame, like a bicycle, with a seat and two skis instead of wheels.

Skijoring
Skiing while being towed.

Slalom
A race in which competitors ski downhill in and out of poles called gates.

Snowboarding
Using a board instead of skis.

Snowmobile
A motorized snow vehicle.

Tuck position
A crouched position used in downhill racing in speed skiing and in ski jumping.

Index